CHURCHILL'S DOG HANDLER, WAS PRESCRIBED A TRANQUILIZER

SUDIPTA KOUSHIK SARMAH

About The Author

Sudipta is a 32 year old commercial banker from Assam, who enjoys reading poetry, non-fiction and appreciates Indian English works of fiction. He takes an interest in long drives, fragrances and good deals on vintage watches. Friends might term him as aloof, and he hopes he has no foes. A devoted husband and doting father of a toddler, holds strong opinions on almost any subject; and lives life with his head held high. Thoroughly enjoys discussions on finance, markets, economics and politics. He is often found asleep comfortably at the destination, having thoroughly enjoyed the journey. Has been wrestling with an unyielding black dog for almost two decades, so people who know him well have seen a lot of nasty bites and scratches.

"There is no terror in the bang, but only in the anticipation of it."

—Alfred Hitchcock (Director)

"Lemon, what happened in your childhood to make you believe people are good?

—Jack Donaghy (30 Rock)

"If fate doesn't make you laugh, you just don't get the joke."

—Gregory David Roberts (in Shantaram)

About The Book

A collection of poems by a person who prefers to speak less, write more. The Churchillian black dog has bitten and scratched him for years and hence, most of the poems in this collection are not uplifting, some might be downright depressing. Poems are anyways not written by happy people, by successful lovers or people who had a happy childhood. So by nature, they are supposed to be gloomy. These poems have been written over 10+ years, re-written and re-hashed numerous times to make the poet not feel embarrassed by his own writing. However, the themes and the hues have remained intact over the constant re-iterations. The poems are in no particular order, by theme, chronology or maturity. The author is simply looking to see if readers feel the inclination to finish the book once they have started.

Contents

Contents

Sudipta Koushik Sarmah

<u>The Stranger in My House</u>

I thought I had killed him last night,
I had thought the same many times before.
Till my neighbor met me on my morning trail,
And said that I looked fresh and well-rested.
So I must have slept last night,
And he must have escaped again.
I have the feeling I saw him in the morning,
But the bedsheet is bloodstained.
I must brush off the events of last night,
And I hope I come back to an empty house.
But when I turn off the steam, showering in
the evening,
He might smile from the mirror again.
I will have to hurry up my dinner,
And maybe skip my nightcap;
Otherwise time will just keep flowing,
Like water from a leaking municipality tap.

Love and Longing
in Mumbai

Staring into the dark abyss that is the cloudy
Mumbai sky,
I fight the pangs of loneliness, with my
paddle-footed cat;
Dipping his claw in the puddle,
Made by the dirt and my tears.

I am afraid my fears have been washed
away by the stinking sea,
But can the burning acid rain wash away
my tears?
The child who fears the night in Mumbai sleeps
soundly,
While I lie wide awake in Bombay.

Does this city ever sleep?
It's five in the morning, and the stoneman
is going to bed,
His wife packing up her lunch for the day,
Salted cucumber and untoasted bread.

Sudipta Koushik Sarmah

The joggers are out in the park,
Earphones plugged in wireless, while;
Some are busy meditating,
After having spent the night with a stranger's
wife.

<u>*Writer's Block – I*</u>

When words cry like a lost child,
And poetry lies...
On crumpled paper, scribbled in blue,
green and black dye;
The pen finally lets out a heaving sigh,
No, the master is not attaining salvation
tonight.

Sudipta Koushik Sarmah

<u>*Offspring*</u>

It's the last day, the year is finally
withering away;
Leaving behind spring's sweet fragrances
and pollen stains;
It will pass by midnight, into the arms of the
decades gone by,
And like always, leaving behind only an
offspring to blame.

<u>*Desolate Girl &*</u>
<u>*Unsuitable Lad*</u>

It surely wasn't love that bound them together,
Might have been the comfort of shared
loneliness;
Or maybe the excesses of pleasure.
Love though, was a symbol of hope,
Probably a paradise that was never to be had,
A desolate girl & an unsuitable lad.

Sudipta Koushik Sarmah

A Casual Conversation in Casualty Ward

*The nurse looks at me with the kind of
hopelessness,
That tells me she's trying to understand, but
despises me nonetheless.
And I seem to have forgotten all but the
white,
The snow that led the way to the charcoal
night.
She's startled me, asking me if I have family
or kin,
Was I loved enough?
She thinks only neglect and spite can lead to
this kind of decay,
I want to tell her the truth, answer the
question no one has asked me till today;
"No ma'am, only the high", I say.*

<u>Not to be a Poet</u>

Don't become a poet, no don't even try to be,
And if you still must, just know,
That you won't ever adorn covers of magazines;
Or ever headline literary fests,
It's not that easy.

Poetry is pretentious snobbery,
That only snobs act like they can understand;
But the masses won't even pretend,
And poetry is dead by now, if you have to ask me.

I made the mistake, and have lived in a one room
kitchen ever since,
Out of the city bounds,
I don't care by now,
If my writing is called shallow, or termed
profound.

Keep writing if you must, but the day you
are over living a hopeless lie,
You have to accept the truth, that poetry is
where writers go to die.

Sudipta Koushik Sarmah

<u>*Waste for Recycling*</u>

*It's difficult to reach for the stars hanging from
the night sky,
With a noose around your neck, for if you step
too far; you die.
The stars for us are just stark reminders,
Of the fact that the day we are born, we already
know,
That they can never be ours.*

*Their parents read them fairy tales, while they
are lovingly tucked in to sleep,
But we are not supposed to dream,
And even if we do, our parents will have to sell
them for rationed kerosene.*

*And they will grow up, 'scum beget scum' they
will say,
And we will live in fear, of being sent for
recycling any day.*

<u>*Stars & Fairytales*</u>

I hope lovers somewhere on Earth tonight,
Will stare at the moon and wonder;
Why the stars do not entice them anymore,
While fairy tales upon, they never hesitate to
ponder.

Sudipta Koushik Sarmah

<u>Judgement Day</u>

Don't tell me what to do, please do not
tell me again,
For every time I seem to be winning;
Life goes ahead, and changes its play.

I hope Charon at least waits for me by
the river,
I hope at least he does not make me wait;
When I land there on my judgement day.

<u>*Dichotomy of Nightmares*</u>

When you sleep tonight, please do not dare to
dream,
For if you sleep light, you might be woken up,
And you may wake up and scream.

When nightmares creep into your bed, into your
blankets,
And eat into your head,
Or slither across the cold floor, leaving the
marble dripping wet.

Or unrested spirits might hide behind the
curtains,
Even though they do not need to;
And hide from those banshees that they
don't like,
The banshees after all, trouble everyone who
sleeps light.

Sudipta Koushik Sarmah

Train Love

Aisle seat of a Mumbai-bound train,
Was reading a pre-owned paperback,
Lost in the protagonist's second-hand pain.
Looked up from my book and there she was,
Typing away on her cellphone, fiddling with her
thin chain;
I knew she might be seeing someone,
But she looked like she needed help,
I felt that I must introduce myself.
I spoke to her, she seemed a bit interested,
She looked towards me and said, "Bhaiya..."
I definitely do not remember the rest,
Till date I tell myself it was for the best,
But still, it caused me momentary pain,
I felt like my train love was lost in vain.

<u>Dead and Breathing</u>

I told them that I was dying,
In fact I told them that I was not even sure,
If I had been dead for a while...
They did not seem to believe me,
They had observed me they said;
That I had been breathing for a very long time.

Sudipta Koushik Sarmah

<u>*Writer's Block – II*</u>

I pick up my pen, still unable to put it to paper,
I desperately need a heartbreak,
I check the newspapers of last week,
If some loved one has been lost at sea,
no obituary of late.

Maybe someone can break my heart, or give
me a reason not to be,
But right now, any words are lost on me.
I need a deceitful lover to be mine,
And then leave, like she left last time,
And then text me, that she reached home fine.

I have tried coffee, whisky and wine,
It's afternoon, soon going to be night;
I need whisky again, to stir my sleeping thoughts,
Or I stand to lose this battle, that I have so long
valiantly fought.

As of now I only feel tired, not high nor awake,
Afterall, I have been trying to write for writing's
sake.

<u>*Clouds on the Horizon*</u>

Clouds are on the horizon, bubblegum pink,
The sky spitting fire, into the darkness
descending,
As if trying to stop an unholy intruder.

The wind whispers a lullaby, a storm is
approaching,
We will hear weeping by the night, when clouds
descend;
As she bids a tearful goodbye to the summer.

Sudipta Koushik Sarmah

<u>*Victory*</u>

When you pass by this long-dead tree stump
someday in future,
You will find our names still engraved;
Your name and mine, white on brown;
And I think that I would want you to stop and
stare,
But I am hopeful, that a little hand would tug at
your shawl that day,
And I know that you will move on, still being able
to call it a victory.

<u>*Grey Christmas*</u>

I sometimes feel dejected, after judging
too much,
Which mars every judgement that I could
perceive;
When my emotions only look to deceive,
Strip me of achievements that I can never
achieve.
Including muddy paths furrowed in Christmas
snow,
As winter sadness comes and then goes,
Only to return with the twilight glow.
The twinkling lights fail to lift my spirits,
Because invitations are already out for new year,
And a lonely Christmas is still my greatest fear.
My eyes burn at the touch of warm water,
Like my cheeks used to crumple when I was a kid;
At the touch of my mother's cold cream,
Tonight it looks like I will have trouble falling
asleep,
Christmas and New Years Eve need to go their
own way,
While I am busy counting imaginary sheep.

Sudipta Koushik Sarmah

<u>*Dead Poet Upstairs*</u>

The poet who lived upstairs was found dead,
The one room kitchen flat still reeking of cheap
cigarettes,
A few drops of Old Monk left in the bottle, still
glistening red.
The cursor still blinking, laptop still on,
Battery low, but cursed and undead.
Few pages lay crumpled on the floor,
Scribbled across in red, blue and black,
And his worn out clothes on the floor, caught
in a cursed roll.
He lay head down on the mattress, cause of
death unknown,
Probably hunger, food poisoning or suicide,
And people who don't read anymore.

<u>*The Blanks*</u>

The blanks don't speak anymore,
With those who look only at words for
inspiration;
Or at fonts for effective persuasion.
The blanks don't speak anymore,
To poets, who criticize wrong punctuation;
Or writers who justify their desperation,
With nothing else but,
The right to freedom of expression.

Sudipta Koushik Sarmah

<u>*We Don't Speak Ill*</u>
<u>*of the Dead*</u>

*We don't speak ill of the dead, lest they be
not at peace,
Because words hurt, and I know my words hurt
them when they were alive;
I don't speak ill of my father who died in his sleep,
Of cancer, I had no idea that he was suffering;
Since years before he died, we had already
stopped talking.
I don't speak ill of my teacher who died of
cirrhosis,
Even though he had always scolded me;
Probably hoping I did not turn out like him.
I don't speak ill of my boss who died of a stroke,
He taught me to manage everything, except my
life;
And now my marriage is falling apart like his.
I will speak no ill of my wife as I bear her no ill
will,
We can hate only those who we once loved.*

Churchill's Dog Handler

*Probably we don't speak ill of the dead, since
we all die the same,
Barely alive, already a foot in the grave,
And we wish nobody speaks ill of us then.*